AN ELEGANT ABC BOOK OF FLOWERS

R IS FOR ROSE

ANTLER & BONE

ISBN: 978-1-966417-47-7 (PRINT)

PUBLISHED BY ANTLER & BONE. ANTLER & BONE'S TITLES MAY BE PURCHASED IN BULK FOR EDUCATIONAL, BUSINESS, FUNDRAISING, OR SALES PROMOTIONAL USE. FOR INFORMATION, PLEASE EMAIL HELLO@ANTLERANDBONE.COM

FIRST PRINT EDITION: 2026

ANTLER & BONE
WWW.ANTLERANDBONE.COM

THIS BOOK
BELONGS TO:
(YOUR NAME)

A
IS FOR
AZALEA

B
IS FOR
BLUEBELL

C
IS FOR
COLUMBINE

D
IS FOR
DAFFODIL

E
IS FOR
ECHINACEA

F
IS FOR
FOXGLOVE

G
IS FOR
GARDENIA

H
IS FOR
HYDRANGEA

I
IS FOR
IRIS

J
IS FOR
JASMINE

K
IS FOR
KINGCUP

L
IS FOR
LAVENDER

M
IS FOR
MARIGOLD

N
IS FOR
NOLANA

O
IS FOR
ORCHID

P
IS FOR
PEONY

Q
IS FOR
QUEEN'S
WREATH

R
IS FOR
ROSE

S
IS FOR
SNAPDRAGON

T
IS FOR
TULIP

U
IS FOR
URSINIA

V
IS FOR
VIOLET

W
IS FOR
WISTERIA

X
IS FOR
XERANTHEMUM

Y
FOR
YARROW

Z
IS FOR
ZINNIA

SHOP ANTLER & BONE'S
PICTURE BOOKS
EXPAND YOUR CHILD'S LIBRARY
WITH BEAUTIFUL AND HIGHLY UNIQUE
CHILDREN'S PICTURE BOOKS.
SHOP OUR VAST CATALOG TODAY!
WWW.ANTLERANDBONE.COM

FREE BOOK GIVEAWAY
EACH MONTH
EVERY MONTH WE ARE CHOOSING A LUCKY READER TO WIN A FREE BOOK.
JUST CREATE AN ACCOUNT AT THE LINK BELOW TO ENTER FOR A CHANCE TO WIN.
ANTLERANDBONE.COM/FREE

www.ingramcontent.com/pod-product-compliance
Lightning Source LLC
LaVergne TN
LVHW070203110826
845147LV00002B/490

* 9 7 8 1 9 6 6 4 1 7 4 7 7 *